T0196063

HOW TO WIN A SOUL
TO CHRIST
and MAKE IT A LIFESTYLE

MAKING SOUL WINNING EASY

LINDA D. CASRAISS

WESTBOW
PRESS®
A DIVISION OF THOMAS NELSON
& ZONDERVAN

WestBow Press books may be ordered through booksellers or by contacting:

WestBow Press
A Division of Thomas Nelson & Zondervan
1663 Liberty Drive
Bloomington, IN 47403
www.westbowpress.com
1 (866) 928-1240

ISBN: 978-1-9736-0530-0 (sc)
ISBN: 978-1-9736-0531-7 (e)

Library of Congress Control Number: 2017916671

Print information available on the last page.

WestBow Press rev. date: 1/9/2018

Special Dedications

I dedicate this book to my Daddy-God, and to my Elder Brother, My Lord and Savior Jesus Christ, and to His precious Holy Spirit who inspired me to write this book.

I send my love to my daughter Shaune' G. Banks and my two grandsons, Xavier C. B. Casraiss and River J. Banks. I thank God for you every day. God loves you and has a great plan for your lives.

To the Editor and my spiritual daughter, LaToya M. Doster. Thank you for your time and sacrifice in editing this book with two small children and one on the way. Many thanks for your work of excellence as unto the LORD on my behalf. Great blessings and rewards to you young lady. I appreciate you !

My favorite Scripture:

Romans 1:16a (KJV)- "For I am not ashamed of the gospel of Christ: for it is the power of God unto salvation to everyone that believeth..."

Contents

CHAPTER 1
The Great Commission

Mark 16:15 (NKJV)

¹⁵ And HE (JESUS) said to them, "Go into all the world and preach the gospel to every creature."

What is the Gospel of Christ? The Gospel of Christ includes the Virgin birth, the death, burial and resurrection of Christ.

Romans 1:16 (NKJV)

¹⁶ "For I am not ashamed of the **gospel of Christ, for it is the power of God** to salvation for everyone who believes, for the Jew first and also for the Greek."

Matthew 28:16-20 (NIV)

¹⁶Then the eleven disciples went to Galilee, to the mountain where Jesus had told them to go. ¹⁷ When they saw him, they worshiped him; but some doubted. ¹⁸ Then Jesus came to them and said, "All authority in heaven and on earth has been given to me. ¹⁹ **Therefore go and make disciples of all nations**, baptizing them in the name of the Father and of the Son and of the Holy Spirit, ²⁰ and **teaching them to obey everything I have commanded you**. And surely, I am with you always, to the very end of the age.

<u>Ponder on these questions:</u>

What does this mean to you? The Great Commission!

How did you get saved? Who led you to Christ? Do you remember the exact day and time?

Were you approached by someone?

Have you ever been given a tract on Salvation?

Have you ever led someone to Christ? If your answer to this question is 'No', then you really need to read this book.

If God told you that for every soul you led to Christ, HE would give you $1,000, you would be winning souls or trying to win souls all day long. That would become a job for you with that kind of income. One thousand dollars per soul! Of course, a soul is worth far more to GOD than $1,000.

Well, the Bible tells us that all heaven rejoices (has a party) when one soul repents giving their life to Christ. We want to cause an ongoing party in heaven leading souls to Christ as a lifestyle !

CHAPTER 2
God's Compassion for the Lost

Let's look at how GOD feels about finding something that is lost.

The Parable of the Lost Sheep

Luke 15:1–7 (NIV) (also found in Matthew 18:12–14 NIV)

[1]Now the tax collectors and sinners were all gathering around to hear Jesus. [2]But the Pharisees and the teachers of the law muttered, "This man welcomes sinners and eats with them." [3]Then Jesus told them this parable: [4]"Suppose one of you has a hundred sheep and loses one of them. Doesn't he leave the ninety-nine in the open country and go after the lost sheep until he finds it? [5]And when he finds it, he joyfully puts it on his shoulders [6]and goes home. Then he calls his friends and neighbors together and says, 'Rejoice with me; I have found my lost sheep.' [7]I tell you that in the same way there will be more rejoicing in heaven over one sinner who repents than over ninety-nine righteous persons who do not need to repent.

The Parable of the Lost Coin

Luke 15:8–10 (NIV)

[8]"Or suppose a woman has ten silver coins and loses one. Doesn't she light a lamp, sweep the house and search carefully until she finds it?

⁹And when she finds it, she calls her friends and neighbors together and says, 'Rejoice with me; I have found my lost coin.' ¹⁰In the same way, I tell you, there is rejoicing in the presence of the angels of God over one sinner who repents."

Surely, a sheep, which represents us, is more important to God to be found or saved much more than a coin.

CHAPTER 3

Pray and Ask God For His Heart's Desires

Psalm 2:8 (NKJV)

"⁸Ask of *Me*, and I will give *You* the nations for your inheritance, And the ends of the earth for *Your* possession."

Let me share this dream with you...The night that 9/11 took place, in a dream I could hear souls crying out from beneath. I knew that those souls, that I could hear, had fallen into hell. It was so vividly clear and loud that it had stirred me out of my sleep. I got out the bed and looked out the window because it sounded so close to me. Then I realized that God was letting me hear the many souls that died that day and were unsaved. This dream gave me more of a hunger to lead souls to Christ.

We should pray Psalm 2:8 and make it a personal prayer for ourselves to have a desire within our hearts to win souls for Christ.

TAKE THAT SCRIPTURE *PERSONALLY*!

Every believer is commanded to save souls:

Matthew 28:18–20 (MSG)

[18-20] Jesus, undeterred, went right ahead and gave his charge: "God authorized and commanded me to commission you: Go out and train everyone you meet, far and near, in this way of life, marking them by baptism in the threefold name: Father, Son, and Holy Spirit. Then instruct them in the practice of all I have commanded you. I'll be with you as you do this, day after day after day, right up to the end of the age.

Most of us are not and have not been accepted by our families after we have gotten saved. And our family members do not want us to preach to them. This was the case between my mother and I. This is my story! My mother did not accept me when I got saved. She thought I was in a cult since she raised me Catholic but I left the Catholic Church. I learned later, that there are many born-again believers in the Catholic Church. She just would not accept the fact that I was not smoking cigarettes, partying, and doing the worldly things that I used to do.

I was raising my daughter in Christ and going to church and Bible Study consistently. We got baptized in a lake, and I invited my mom and her friends. Her friends thought it was great but she still frowned upon it, since it was not what she was used to. Nevertheless, she never found joy in my changed life. It seemed to intimidate her. I love her and treated her as though she was saved, knowing that she had not accepted Christ into her heart- yet. I still receive some indifference even when I am around her. I stopped talking to her about Christ; I just loved her like Christ.

Mom passed in December 2016 at the age of 87. During the last three months of my mother's life the Lord revealed to me that she had accepted Him into her life as her personal Savior. Two months before my mom went into the hospital I had a dream. In the dream, I saw her sitting up in the bed next to her mother, my grandmother (I led my grandmother to Christ) and both of them were looking up. At that time, I did not understand what the Lord was showing me, what He was telling me, and certainly not that the dream would soon come to pass. Nevertheless, during the final months of my mom's life, God bonded us together as one in such a loving and graceful way. I remained at her side during her surgery. Myself and so many others prayed for her recovery since the doctor did not think she would make it through the next few days. She recovered enough to go into rehab, and a few days later God sent an angel for her and took her to be with Him. HE told me that HE sent an angel for her. So, you can be confident and encouraged that the most stubborn person in your family that resists getting saved will someday give their life to Christ because of your prayers and your witness. Live God's love before them. It works!

I just want to encourage you never give up on your loved ones. Mom had beat cancer at 80 years old, and survived a fall on the casino escalator where her bone protruded out of her leg. And this surgery was no easy feat! So, God's hand was on her life all along.

This is my testimony! When I got saved I left my unsaved friends completely. They said I thought I was better than them, but it wasn't that at all. I just stopped what I was doing while they were still doing drugs, drinking, smoking, partying, etc. I stopped doing all of those things, except smoking pot. But, after five years of being saved, one of my old friends called me and said that they all thought wrong. They realized that I was sincere about living for the LORD and apologized for their thinking. One day, a friend called me, and I invited her and her husband to church. Soon after that, her husband gave his life to Christ and was totally delivered from heroine. Sadly, my girlfriend was jealous of his walk with GOD and gave him a hard time. To this day I don't know if she has truly given her life to the LORD.

I said I gave up everything but smoking pot. I knew it was illegal, but I never thought about it as being sin. So, one Sunday I left out the church, lit a joint on the church steps, took my first puff and hopped in my car and drove off. Sister 'so and so' came right out the door behind me and she smelled the pot. Seeing me drive off, she knew I had been smoking and ran right to the pastor and told on me!

That evening the pastor called me at home, even though she never mentioned why she was calling, I knew why. During the phone call, she never condemned me and she never made me feel bad. She ministered to me in the love of Christ. She began to talk to me about my body being the temple of the Holy Ghost. I got my bible and we read 1 Corinthians 6:19 (KJV) together: "**What? know ye not that your body is the temple of the Holy Ghost which is in you, which ye have of God, and ye are not your own**?"

After we prayed together, I took that nickel bag of weed that I had and flushed it down the toilet and I have never smoked pot since and that was 35 years ago. That was the power of the Holy Ghost and love!

Share your testimonies as much as you can. They will encourage you and others "[11] **And they overcame him by the blood of the Lamb, and by the word of their testimony; and they loved not their lives unto the death**" (Rev. 12:11, KJV). We all need to encourage ourselves sometimes with what we know is true and about what GOD has already done for us.

FAMILY FIRST

Ministering to family first is part of the Great Commission. After that, you just have to pray for them and trust GOD. You have already planted the seed.

Psalm 37:4 (KJV)

[4] Delight thyself also in the LORD: and he shall give thee the desires of thine heart.

Seeing our family saved is a desire of our hearts and GOD will do it. Make winning souls for Christ a desire of your heart. Ask the LORD to give you a burden for souls. Ask HIM to make winning souls to Christ your heart's desire. Ask HIM that until you are actually doing it. Winning souls to Christ and being conscientious that you have natural awareness of their NEED, their GREAT NEED for CHRIST. Pray for this daily until it becomes a lifestyle.

Are you afraid to walk up to someone and talk to them about Christ? Here's what you can do:

1. Write your fears down.
2. Discuss the fears of doing this in a public place with a friend.
3. **Pray about your fears together with someone you know and trust!**
4. Take authority over them.
5. Pick someone that may like to go Soulwinning with you.

CHAPTER 4

How to Approach People

Introducing yourself. Smile. Be Friendly. State your name. Give a handshake. Give a compliment:

Example: "Hi! I am (your first name). Has anyone ever told you that GOD loves you and has a wonderful plan for your life?"

You may get a NO response and then you can proceed sharing that GOD loves them and that's why they met you. Or go right into sharing the love of GOD for them.

If you get a YES response, ask them, **"On a scale from 1 to 10, where would you say your walk with Christ is**?" If it is a 5 or less, you need to share the importance of being on fire for God and pray with them that the fire of God falls upon them.

More ways to approach:

1) Start a conversation about the weather, family, economy, finances, general things, ultimately letting the person or people know that you want to talk to them about the LOVE of GOD. Never tell anyone that they are going to hell.

Ask if they have a prayer request —usually a response at that point is their finances or their health. Use that as an opportunity and allow the power of the Holy Ghost to minister to them whether they say the sinner's prayer or not. Let the LORD use you right then.

2) At some point ask, "Who do you trust?" They may have been hurt by someone they trusted. Let them know that GOD is trustworthy and why.

CHAPTER 5
Need to Know Scriptures

Scriptures on planting seed, watering seed and GOD giving the increase.

1 Corinthians 3:6 (AMP) [6] I planted, Apollos[1] watered, but God [all the while] was making it grow and [He] gave the increase.

1 Corinthians 3:6 (NIV) [6] I planted the seed, and Apollos watered it, but it was God who made it grow.

1 Corinthians 3:6 (MSG) [6] I planted, Apollos watered, but God gave the growth.

1 Corinthians 3:7 (NIV) [7] So neither the one who plants nor the one who waters is anything, but only God, who makes things grow.

1 Corinthians 3:7 (NLT) [7] It's not important who does the planting, or who does the watering. What's important is that God makes the seed grow.

(I like this translation the best!) 1 Corinthians 3:5-9 (MSG) "[5-9] Who do you think Paul is, anyway? Or Apollos, for that matter?

---

[1] This makes reference to a follower of Jesus Christ, Apollos. He is mentioned in Acts 18:24: "Meanwhile a Jew named Apollos, a native of Alexandria, came to Ephesus. He was an eloquent man, well versed in the Scriptures."

Servants, both of us—servants who waited on you as you gradually learned to entrust your lives to our mutual Master. We each carried out our servant assignment. I planted the seed, Apollos watered the plants, but God made you grow. It's not the one who plants or the one who waters who is at the center of this process but God, who makes things grow. Planting and watering are menial servant jobs at minimum wages. What makes them worth doing is the God we are serving. You happen to be God's field in which we are working."

So, this scripture takes the weight off of you. You are not the one who saves. JESUS SAVES! HE gets the credit and all the GLORY! The work is the work of the Holy Spirit! People that you approach may have been prepared before even meeting you.

THIS IS YOUR DAY! The seed has already been planted and watered and the individual's soul is ripe and ready to receive Christ upon your approach and BAM! You happen to say all the right things and lead them into the sinner's prayer, and that soul repents and receives CHRIST into their life. REJOICE! That is the greatest feeling in the world. It is the most rewarding and all of heaven rejoices over that soul that just gave their life to Christ (Lk. 15:10, NIV). You have received a soul winner's crown!

CHAPTER 6
Crowns

We did learn from Romans 14, one encouraging thing. When God judges the secrets of men, the counsels of the heart, every man shall have praise of God. There will be a reward of some sort for everyone. Thank God! The Holy Spirit is pleased to describe these rewards as crowns[2].

(The following scriptures can be taken from any bible translation of the reader's choosing.)

1) <u>**The Five Crowns of Salvation**</u>
   a. The Crown of Life (Jas. 1:12)
   b. The Incorruptible Crown (1 Cor. 9:25)
   c. The Crown of Righteousness (2 Tim. 4:8)
   d. The Crown of Glory (1 Pet. 5:4)
   e. The Crown of Exultation/ Rejoicing (1 Thess. 2:19 -The Soul Winner's Crown)

We are reminded that God has crowns available for every individual. We are also reminded that we should be very careful that someone else does not receive the crown that was intended for us. This is explained in Revelations 3:11 (NIV): **"I am coming soon. Hold on to what you have, so that no one will take your crown."**

---

[2] Dr. Joe Temple **Crown of Rejoicing: Soul-Winner's Crown** http://www.livingbiblestudies.org/study/JT2/003.html

We are reminded that after we have begun the work, that we complete the job so that we may receive a full reward. This is also explained in 2 John 1:8 (NLT) "**Watch out that you do not lose what we have worked hard to achieve. Be diligent so that you received your full reward.**"

We learned that after we receive the crowns, we are going to have the happy privilege of casting them at the feet of the Lord Jesus Christ, as we cry out from the very depths of our hearts "**Worthy art Thou, O Lord**" (Rev. 4:11, KJV). We will not be able to talk about our own worthiness.

CHAPTER 7

Guaranteed Resistance and Rejection

What helped me in this situation and how I overcame the rejection is not only did I have to figure out how to overcome the rejection, but I sought the LORD to give me an answer to share with others how to deal with the rejection and those who shun or flag or rush off as to not want to be bothered or even continue to listen to what you have to say.

This is what the LORD told me a Rhema word to help me: "Linda, those souls that are assigned to you will stop and listen and will receive what you have to tell them- with a little persistence. Those not assigned to you will keep on going. Someone else will minister to them." This totally relieved me of the rejection that I was encountering and really feeling bad that I was not doing the right thing, saying the right things, etc. Perhaps this will be helpful to you: Receive in your heart that those souls that just will not give you the time of day are assigned to someone else. Keep a smile and be friendly and remember that and move on to the next soul that is assigned to you. The LORD knows where you are, when you will be there, and everyone else that will be there too. You will get a nudging in your spirit to speak to the next person at the gas pump, or in the grocery store line, or passing someone pushing their cart next to yours, or when your neighbors bump into you, etc. Some of you have probably felt that nudge and ignored it. Do

NOT ignore it anymore. The GOD of Abraham, Isaac and Jacob wants to use you. YES YOU! You could lead the next Joshua to Christ, or the next Moses, or the next Billy Graham, or the next great Prophet or Prophetess to Christ. It's exciting and you will reap great rewards.

CHAPTER 8
Soul Winning Scriptures

Romans 6:23 (KJV)

"For the wages of sin is death; but the gift of God is eternal life in Jesus Christ our Lord."

1-What are wages? Wages, according to Webster: a payment usually of money for labor or services usually for an hourly, daily basis. (i.e. Payment for sin is death)

2-What is a gift? Gift-Something voluntarily transferred by one person to another without compensation. The act, right, or power of giving.

Really understanding what Jesus did by giving us a free gift makes us want to give Jesus to someone else and tell others about this gift of eternal life.

You do not or did not have to work for this gift or try hard to get it-Jesus gave Himself freely. Salvation is a free gift from GOD.

Romans 10:1(KJV)

"For whosoever shall call upon the name of the Lord shall be saved."

The person needs to know that they are a WHOSOEVER.

JUST LIKE YOU !

Romans 10:9-10 (NIV)

[9]If you declare with your mouth, "Jesus is Lord," and believe in your heart that God raised him from the dead, you will be saved. [10] For it is with your heart that you believe and are justified, and it is with your mouth that you profess your faith and are saved.

Romans 10:9-10 (NKJV)

[9]If you confess with your mouth the Lord Jesus and believe in your heart that God has raised Him from the dead, you will be saved. [10] For with the heart one believes unto righteousness, and with the mouth confession is made unto salvation.

Romans 10:4-10 (MSG)

"[4-10]The earlier revelation was intended simply to get us ready for the Messiah, who then puts everything right for those who trust him to do it. Moses wrote that anyone who insists on using the law code to live right before God soon discovers it's not so easy—every detail of life regulated by fine print! But trusting God to shape the right living in us is a different story—no precarious climb up to heaven to recruit the Messiah, no dangerous descent into hell to rescue the Messiah. So, what exactly was Moses saying? The word that saves is right here, as near as the tongue in your mouth, as close as the heart in your chest. It's the word of faith that welcomes God to go to work and set things right for us. This is the core of our preaching. Say the welcoming word to God—"Jesus is my Master"—embracing, body and soul, God's work of doing in us what he did in raising Jesus from the dead. That's it. That's salvation. You're not "doing" anything;

you're simply calling out to God, trusting him to do it for you. With your whole being you embrace."

God setting things right, and then you say it, right out loud: "**God has set everything right between him and me!**"

A COMPLETED REDEMPTIVE WORK!

CHAPTER 9
God's Plan of Salvation

1 John 5:11-12 (NKJV)

"¹¹ And this is the testimony: God has given us eternal life, and this life is in His Son. ¹² He who has the SON has eternal LIFE; he who does not have the SON of GOD does not have life."

This passage tells us that GOD has given us eternal LIFE and this LIFE is in HIS SON JESUS CHRIST. In other words, the way to possess eternal life is to possess GOD'S SON. The question is how can a person have the SON OF GOD?"

Man's Problem----Separation from GOD

Isaiah 59:2 (NET)

² But your sinful acts have alienated you from your GOD; your sins have caused HIM to reject you and not listen to your prayers.

Romans 5:8 (NIV)

"⁸ But GOD demonstrates HIS love for us in this: While we were still sinners, Christ died for us."

Why did JESUS have to die for us? Because Scripture declares all men to be sinful. To "sin," means to miss the mark. The BIBLE declares, "**...all have sinned and fallen or come short of the glory (the perfect holiness) of God**" (Rom.3:23, NKJV). In other words, our sin separates us from GOD who is perfect holiness (righteousness and justice) and GOD must therefore judge sinful man. GOD is too just to tolerate evil and HE is unable to condone wrong doing.

Ephesians 2:1(KJV)

[1] And you hath he quickened, who were dead in trespasses and sins...

Romans 6:23 (NIV)

[23] For the wages of sin is death, but the gift of God is eternal life through Jesus Christ our Lord.

HOLY GOD-ETERNAL LIFE

John 17:3 (NIV)

[3] Now this is eternal life: that they know you, the only true GOD, and Jesus Christ, whom you have sent.

Scripture also teaches that there is no amount to human goodness, human works or human morality, or religious activity can gain acceptance with GOD or get anyone into heaven. The moral man, the religious man, the immoral man and the non-religious are all in the same boat. They all fall short of GOD'S perfect righteousness. After discussing the immoral man, the moral man, and the righteous man in Romans 1:18, 3:8, the Apostle Paul declares that both the Jew and the Greek are under sin, "As it is written: There is no one righteous, not even one" (Rom. 3:10, NIV).

Make your own "hint" cards.

You may use info on ANY PAGE to make YOUR OWN note cards for soul winning and keep the cards handy in your wallet to use when needed.

Get excited and use the Bible for references and be creative with your Hint cards.

CHAPTER 10

Repentance: You Need to Know That There IS A DIFFERENCE in

True Repentance and Insincere Repentance

Example of true repentance: Psalm 51(NKJV): A Prayer of Repentance

A Psalm of David when Nathan the prophet went to him, after he had gone in to Bathsheba.

Have mercy upon me, O God,
According to Your loving kindness;
According to the multitude of Your tender mercies,
Blot out my transgressions.
² Wash me thoroughly from my iniquity,
And cleanse me from my sin.
³ For I acknowledge my transgressions,
And my sin is always before me.
⁴ Against You, You only, have I sinned,
And done this evil in Your sight—
That You may be found just when You speak,
And blameless when You judge.
⁵ Behold, I was brought forth in iniquity,
And in sin my mother conceived me.

⁶ Behold, You desire truth in the inward parts,

And in the hidden part You will make me to know wisdom.

⁷ Purge me with hyssop, and I shall be clean;

Wash me, and I shall be whiter than snow.

⁸ Make me hear joy and gladness,

That the bones You have broken may rejoice.

⁹ Hide Your face from my sins,

And blot out all my iniquities.

¹⁰ Create in me a clean heart, O God,

And renew a steadfast (a right) spirit within me.

¹¹ Do not cast me away from Your presence,

And do not take Your Holy Spirit from me.

¹² Restore to me the joy of Your salvation,

And uphold me by Your generous Spirit.

¹³ Then I will teach transgressors Your ways,

And sinners shall be converted to You.

¹⁴ Deliver me from the guilt of bloodshed, O God,

The God of my salvation,

And my tongue shall sing aloud of Your righteousness.

¹⁵ O Lord, open my lips,

And my mouth shall show forth Your praise.

¹⁶ For You do not desire sacrifice, or else I would give it;

You do not delight in burnt offering.

¹⁷ The sacrifices of God are a broken spirit,

A broken and a contrite heart—

These, O God, You will not despise.

¹⁸ Do good in Your good pleasure to Zion;

Build the walls of Jerusalem.

¹⁹ Then You shall be pleased with the sacrifices of righteousness,

With burnt offering and whole burnt offering;

Then they shall offer bulls on Your altar.

Example of Insincere Repentance: Exodus 9:27-35 (NIV)

[27] Then Pharaoh quickly summoned Moses and Aaron. "This time I have sinned," he confessed. "The LORD is the righteous one, and my people and I are wrong. [28] Please beg the LORD to end this terrifying thunder and hail. We've had enough. I will let you go; you don't need to stay any longer."

[29] "All right," Moses replied. "As soon as I leave the city, I will lift my hands and pray to the LORD. Then the thunder and hail will stop, and you will know that the earth belongs to the LORD. [30] But I know that you and your officials still do not fear the LORD God."

[31] All the flax and barley were ruined by the hail, because the barley had formed heads and the flax was budding. [32] But the wheat and the emmer wheat were spared, because they had not yet sprouted from the ground. [33] So Moses left Pharaoh's court and went out of the city. When he lifted his hands to the LORD, the thunder and hail stopped, and the downpour ceased. [34] But when Pharaoh saw that the rain, hail, and thunder had stopped, he and his officials sinned again, and Pharaoh again became stubborn. [35] Because his heart was hard, Pharaoh refused to let the people leave, just as the LORD had predicted through Moses. Pharaoh lied and his repentance was insincere.

CHAPTER 11

You Have To Know For Yourself That You Must Be Born Again

JUST A LITTLE REVIEW: "You must be born again" (Jn. 3:7, NIV). The religious leader who heard these words first spoken almost 2,000 years ago seemed stunned by them. This man, Nicodemus, a Pharisee and a ruler of the Jews, had already acknowledged his belief that Jesus Christ had come from GOD, "for no one can do these signs that YOU do unless GOD is with him." Chapter three of the Gospel of John records this intriguing conversation between Jesus and Nicodemus giving us a vital key to the kingdom of GOD. Both believers and unbelievers still use Jesus' words "born again," and many, like Nicodemus, are still confused by them.

Nicodemus asked Jesus, "How can a man be born again when he is old? He cannot enter a second time into his mother's womb and be born, can he?" (Jn 3:4, NASB). Nicodemus was thinking in terms of the flesh. Jesus had to explain to him, "*that which is born of the flesh is flesh; and that which is born of the Spirit is spirit. Do not marvel that I said to you, you must be born again.*" (Jn. 3:6-7, ESV). Jesus also explained that unless a person is born again, he cannot see or enter the kingdom of GOD. Obviously, this born-again experience, whatever it is, is absolutely necessary and of the utmost importance. We cannot take it lightly. Also, Jesus said imperatively, "You must...." A COMMAND

FROM THE SON OF GOD. You can imagine the incredulous look on the face of Nicodemus. He couldn't believe such a thing. All his life, he had been taught that good works were the key to heaven – that if a person observed all the laws and requirements of GOD, he would have entrance into heaven. He said to Jesus, "How can these things be?"

You see, Jesus was talking about things of the spirit. He compared the spirit with the wind. You cannot see it; you don't know where it's coming from or where it's going. But it is real, and you see its effects. You hear it. You see what it does to the trees. You see the leaves that are caught up in the wind. You see the little swirls of dust. You feel the wind on your face. Jesus said, "So is everyone who is born of the spirit."

The Flesh vs **The Spirit** The problem was that Nicodemus, like all human beings, was of the flesh. He was from the earth. Flesh is moral. It is subject to death, decay and corruption. It is filled with self-pity, self-pride, self-love. An awesome fact exists about the flesh: everything we see, everything visible, even our own bodies, are perishing. Many people try everything imaginable to ignore or forget this, but the fact always remains. The Bible says that things which are visible are temporary but things which are invisible are eternal. The truth is that we dwell in a mortal body which will soon return to dust. What then of the spirit which lives in the body?

Could this BE You? Assume for a moment that this is you. Your body has returned to dust. Your spirit is carried into the presence of your Creator. There you stand, stripped of all of your possessions, all of your friends, all of your accomplishments. Former titles, salary levels, bank accounts, and club memberships mean nothing.

GOD looks at you with love and compassion, yet in holy and righteous judgment. In that awful moment He asks, "What reason can you give Me to come and spend eternity with Me, in what is called heaven?"

"Why, I've lived a good life," you say. Or, "I worked hard and provided for my family." Or, I was a member of a church and I have kept the Ten Commandments" (though only Jesus has kept all the Commandments). Or, "I was a church leader, a Bishop or an Elder, or a Deacon. I was a ministry leader."

You go on and on. And in each instance GOD would shake HIS head and say, "I'm sorry. I love you, but I cannot let you into heaven with Me. You are relying on your good works, and <u>by the works of the flesh shall no man be justified.</u> You must be born again of My Spirit in order to enter heaven."

CHAPTER 12
The Answer

It is clear that our old state, our old nature and even all our good deeds are insufficient. GOD is totally and absolutely holy and righteous. HE is perfect. We cannot fellowship with HIM now or in the next life in the imperfection of our present nature. Perfection and imperfection are incompatible. **"All have sinned and fall short of the glory of GOD** "(Rom. 3:23, NIV). By our very self-seeking nature we are sinful and imperfect. And sin results in death, and eternal separation from GOD. This is a result of our earthly nature. It is obvious that we need a new nature, a nature that GOD can look upon with acceptance. A nature that stands justified before HIM. We need new birth. You must be born again.

A Free Gift: First, it is free, a gift from GOD! We cannot earn it. We cannot work for it or else we could boast, and no one shall boast before GOD. And imperfect creature cannot earn or deserve such a merit from a holy GOD. **"For the wages of sin is death but the free gift of GOD is eternal life in CHRIST JESUS our LORD."** (Rom 6:23, NLT).

This free gift comes to us by grace, or "unmerited favor." Only GOD'S supreme love makes such a free and wonderful gift possible. GOD did not automatically excuse our sinful condition. He paid the greatest price. You see, sin must be punished. GOD in HIS holy and righteous nature must judge sin.

Not to do so would deny HIS very nature. HE Himself has decreed that, "The wages of sin is death."

No Greater Love Than This

The most magnificent and incomparable act of love in all history is that GOD took our sins and death upon Himself. Jesus took the punishment in our place. He became our substitute. "**God made Him who knew no sin to be sin on our behalf, so that we might become the righteousness of GOD in Him Jesus Christ**..." (2 Cor. 5:21, NIV). Although HE existed in the form of GOD, did not regard equality with GOD a thing to be grasped, but emptied Himself, taking the form of a bond-servant, and being made in the likeness of men. And being found in appearance as a man, He humbled Himself by becoming obedient to the point of death, even death on the cross."**For GOD so loved the world, that HE gave HIS only begotten Son, that whosoever believes in HIM should not perish, but have eternal life**" (Jn 3:16,NIV).

This is why Christ chose to die- to make the supreme love gift of taking all of our punishment upon Himself to reconcile the world unto GOD. He totally identified with our sinful nature, and became sin for us though sinless Himself, so that we might have the free gift of forgiveness and life.

The Mystery Solved

The second important fact about this new nature is that it is actually the nature of the only perfect Person who ever lived, Jesus Christ. Only Jesus is good enough. Only He is perfect.

Only His life is acceptable to GOD. It is only as we partake of His Life that we become acceptable to GOD. Being "born again" is nothing less than receiving the actual life of the living Christ- His Spirit actually entering us and bringing our spirit to life. Our spirit is joined with His. "**The one who joins Himself to the Lord is one spirit with Him**" (1 Cor. 6:17,CEB). Then we become one with the perfect One. "**I have been crucified with Christ; it is no longer I who live, but Christ lives in me**" (Gal. 2:20, NKJV). The mystery is now solved, "the riches of the glory of this mystery among the Gentiles: which is Christ in you, the hope of glory." (Col. 1:27, NKJV)

Jesus' identification with us is complete. In His death He bore our sins and suffered our death.

PRAISE BREAK!!!!!

In His resurrection He became our life, so much so that in His Spirit we are even joined with Him. Now when the Father looks upon us He sees only the righteousness of Jesus.

WE ARE ACCEPTED! If no one else accepts you, you are accepted by the Father, GOD. When no one else will talk to you, GOD the Father will talk to you. When you feel that no one else loves you GOD loves you. When you feel that no one else is around or even wants to be around you, GOD is always around you and HE genuinely wants to be around you. We have been born again! "**Therefore, if anyone is in Christ, he is a new creation; the old things passed away; behold, all things have become new**" (2 Cor. 5:17, NKJV).

CHAPTER 13
The Abundant Life Now

The third important fact is that when we are born again, we become a new creature, NOW. The heavenly promise is for the future and will be wonderful beyond understanding. However, at the new birth we begin to experience the life of GOD as He guides us, walks with us and indwells us. We experience the fruit of HIS Spirit such as love, joy and peace. As we are filled with His Spirit we experience the supernatural power manifested in life situations. Life takes on a new meaning. Everything is in a new perspective, Jesus said that He came not just to get us to heaven, but that we "...might have life, and might have it more abundantly" (Jn 10:10, KJV).

CHAPTER 14
How to Receive HIM

The fourth important fact to know is how to receive the gift. Doesn't every act of giving require a giver and a receiver? GOD, the Giver, holds out the gift to everyone. (Good to say when leading a soul to CHRIST). It is not His will that any should perish. NOTE: THIS TOO IS GREAT TO INCLUDE WHEN MINISTERING TO THE LOST. But to receive a gift requires that we **agree** to a need. We must agree as the Spirit of GOD shows us that we are indeed sinful creatures in need of GOD'S forgiveness and grace. **"I tell you, no, but unless you repent, you will all likewise perish"** (Lk.13:5, NASB).

Repentance means to change your mind, to turn. We must change our mind about our condition and our direction away from GOD, and turn to HIM. "But as many as received Him (Christ) to them HE gave the right to become children of GOD". (Include this when leading a soul to Christ). We receive Christ by an ingenious method that only God can devise. It is not by works, because your abilities would vary and everyone would not have an equal chance. It is an ability that is equal regardless of intelligence, sex, age, race, social status or wealth. It is by faith. **"For by grace you have been saved, through faith- and this is not from yourselves, it is the gift of GOD- not a result of works, that no one can boast"** (Ep. 2:8-9, NIV).

To receive Christ we must acknowledge our need and who HE is. (Acknowledging need – important when ministering to an individual– their need for a Savior). Then we simply turn to Him by faith and put our trust and reliance on HIM. We receive Him by invitation. Jesus said, "**Behold, I stand at the door and knock; if anyone hears my voice, and opens the door, I will come in to him, and will dine with him, and he with ME**" (Rev. 3:20, NKJV).

Essential to Say

Do you want to be born again, right now? Do you want a 'new nature'? Do you want to receive the most wonderful gift in the whole universe, the life of GOD Himself?

You may use the following prayer to lead a soul to Christ. Then simply, but sincerely, pray asking the person to repeat after you:

"Dear Lord Jesus, I believe that YOU are the Son of GOD. I believe that YOU died for my sins and rose from the grave. Forgive me of my sin. I invite YOU into my heart and receive YOU right NOW as Lord and Savior of my life! Thank YOU for forgiving me. Thank YOU for a new life. Thank you for saving me. Help me to be what YOU want me to be and live YOUR life through me. Amen."

CHAPTER 15

Here's What's Next

If you sincerely prayed that prayer, GOD says that you have new life/ eternal life and that you are a member of the Kingdom of GOD. He desires close fellowship with you during this life and desires for you even now to live victoriously as a child of the KING! **(NOTE: THIS IS VERY IMPORTANT TO TELL A NEW BELIEVER).**

Also, since He died for you, He wants you to live for Him. "And HE died for all, that they who live should no longer live for themselves, but for Him who died and rose again on their behalf." As we are born again, GOD immediately implants a new nature within us. Some outward change may be dramatic and instant; some may come gradually. As with all newborn, our new nature needs nurture and growth. Talk to Him frequently. And listen to HIS voice within you. That's what prayer is. Read and meditate upon His Word, the BIBLE, which is the greatest way that HE speaks to you. Finally, He wants you to fellowship with other believers and be a functioning part of His Corporate Body. That's what the church is.

What church should you attend? Ask GOD to lead you and He will. **(Invite the person/persons to your church). Get the telephone number of that person or persons so you can follow up on them and meet them at your church when they arrive.**

SCRIPTURES YOU MAY WANT TO LOOK UP AND WRITE DOWN:

(The following scriptures can be taken from any bible translation of the reader's choosing.)

II Corinthians 4:18

II Corinthians 5:17

John 10:10

Romans 3:23

Ephesians2:8-9

II Corinthians 5:21

John 3:16

Colossians 1:26-27

Romans 3:20

Romans 6:23

Philippians 2:6-8

I Corinthians 6:17

Galatians 2:20

<u>Just some to help ya out!</u>

CHAPTER 16
In Your Life as A Believer

Scripture says: "**But the fruit of the Spirit is love, joy, peace, longsuffering, gentleness, goodness, faith, meekness, temperance: against such there is no law**" (Gal. 5:22-23, KJV).

Romans 5:5 (KJV)
[5] **And hope maketh not ashamed; because the love of GOD is shed abroad in our hearts by the Holy Ghost which is given to us.**

John 15:9-13 (KJV)
[9] **As the Father hath loved me, so have I loved you; continue ye in my love. [10] If you keep my commandments, ye shall abide in my love; even as I have kept my Father's commandments, and abide in HIS love. [11] These things I have spoken unto you, that my joy might remain in you, and that your joy might be full. [12] This is my commandment, that ye love one another, as I have loved you. [13] Greater love hath no man than this, that a man lay down his life for his friends.**"

How to love and be loved
When you are born again of the Spirit of GOD, our old nature is changed, and GOD can give you love for others that is greater than normal human love. The Holy Spirit working within you can

produce the highest form of love—AGAPE LOVE. It is the love GOD has for you, wherein HE loves regardless of whether you love Him in return. It is the love you need in order to love others regardless of their response to your love.

The substance of genuine Agape love is not learned, but a product of the Holy Spirit. It is felt emotionally as your heart receives it. You will realize that you also have a genuine love for GOD and want to be a blessing to Him and for Him. You will feel a sense of oneness towards others that can be described as being one in essence, one in spirit, one in purpose and effort, one emotionally, and even one physically (as with a spouse)– but especially one in the Spirit of GOD.

The person who said that, "love is a feeling you feel when you feel like you are going to have a feeling you've never felt before" was describing love as a heartfelt emotion. But **if not acted out**, this emotion cannot be labeled true love. In that sense, it is like faith which if not accompanied by the works which establish it, is not true faith. Great examples of this can be read in Jesus' confrontation with Peter about Peter's love for Him (Jn 21:15-17, NIV), and James' discourse on faith (Ja. 2:17-26, NKJV). Yet an act of love is just so much noise unless it comes from the heart filled with love (1 Cor. 13, NIV). Pray that the Holy Spirit will give you love, the fruit of the Spirit. Ask for the great love for people in general. Then specifically ask for the great love for a person whom you find difficult to love. It is then that your deliberate act of love will be received and recognized as genuine, not just an empty action.

You possess genuine love for someone when you find yourself with the desire to bless that person. Ask GOD to show you all the praiseworthy things about that person and how you can bless him/her. Then look for opportunities to share those praiseworthy things, (a few at a time) and to bless the person. You will soon discover that you genuinely love the person and can soon expect him/her to love you.

Never try and demonstrate your love for someone to impress someone else. That is not the genuine love of GOD for people.

How to overcome barriers- Barriers to love include pride, jealousy, conceit, ill manneredness, irritability, holding grudges, selfishness, evil actions or thoughts, childishness and a "give-up" attitude (1 Cor. 13, NIV). If one or more of these is an obstacle in your life repent and ask GOD to forgive you for your feelings and actions.

Renounce such attitudes and behavior in your life. Begin to praise and thank GOD, who will change your life as you ask Him. He will free you from the depression, anxiety, anger, hate of that "queasy," uneasy feeling in the pit of your stomach caused by the thought or presence of a particular person. As you begin to appreciate (praise, honor, encourage) people, you will find yourself becoming a positive, victorious, successful, loving person. When you depreciate (find fault with, criticize, gossip, etc.) people, you find yourself becoming negative, unloving and unloved. When you are a depreciator, you are often part of the problem rather than part of the solution. People may not desire your company, except those of like attitude.

To overcome lovelessness on your part, ask GOD to produce within you the character traits of truthfulness, faithfulness, hope, patience, spiritual maturity and especially the fruit qualities produced by the Holy Spirit. As you find yourself being transformed, and your mind being renewed (Rom. 12:2, NKJV), you will discover that you are able to get along with anyone and also that anyone can get along with you. The reality of love—the love of GOD within you for Himself and others- will be yours.

However, do not demand to receive love before you love or to have your love returned. Let GOD bring that about. Be faithful in the loving nature that GOD gives you. Pray in agreement with GOD'S word that GOD will fill you with His love and Holy Spirit. Just simply ask the LORD to fill you with His love. And HE will.

GOD gives us HIS love for all people so that we will have a great desire to WIN the lost at any cost. God commends His love to us. He commands us to love Him and our fellow men. God is love and He stands ready to produce His perfect love within us (Gal. 5:22, NKJV). We will know we love God, when we love our brethren in Christ and our fellow men, including our enemies. (1 Jn. 4:19-21, NIV).

LOVE: SCRIPTURES TO LIVE BY
(The following scriptures can be taken from any bible translation of the reader's choosing.)

Read the entire book of 1 John

1 Corinthians 13:4-8 Characteristics associated with love

John 3:16	God's love revealed
1 John 4:/-14	God's love explained
Revelation 1:5	Christ's love is forever
Ephesians 2:4,5	God's love unearned
Matthew 22:37,38	Christ's Command to love
John 13:34,35	Love for each other proves we are God's people
Matthew 5:43,44	Love for enemies

You will know them by their fruit that they have love one for the other (Mt 7:16-20, NIV). This is the only scripture that tells us how we will know another believer. LOVE has to be a lifestyle and loving as GOD loves us-Agape Love! Practice it until it comes natural for you, even though it is supernatural.

CHAPTER 17
Public Places

Some people in public places may respond quicker upon your approach if you ask: "Can I pray for you?" Everyone needs prayer. Especially if you find some resistance, ask the individual person if you can pray for them about something: their finances, their health, their children, their family, and their spouse, etc.

Be able to listen and show compassion.

Matthew 9:35-38 (NKJV): The Compassion of Jesus and a plea from the LORD for us to go after souls!

[35] Then Jesus went about all the cities and villages, teaching in their synagogues, preaching the gospel of the kingdom, and healing every sickness and every disease among the people. [36] But when He saw the multitudes, He was moved with compassion for them, because they were weary and scattered, like sheep having no shepherd. [37] Then He said to His disciples, "The harvest truly is plentiful, but the laborers are few. [38] Therefore, pray the Lord of the harvest to send out laborers into His harvest."

Mark 1:41(NKJV)
[41] Then Jesus, moved with compassion, stretched out His hand and touched him, and said to him, "I am willing; be cleansed."

Matthew 20:34 (NIV)
[34] Jesus had compassion on them and touched their eyes. Immediately they received their sight and followed him.

PRAY for compassion like JESUS – pray this daily until you get it. Pray this for yourselves.

CHAPTER 18
Healing

When someone or yourself has an illness, disease, infirmity or other physical, mental or spiritual problems, you should seek God for healing. God wants you to be whole. HE is sovereign and desires to make His children vessels fit for good works. He wants you healed and whole until He takes away your breath at His appointed time (Ps. 104:29, NIV). In fact, Jesus bore your stripes in His body so that you might be healed (Isa. 53:5, NKJV).

Steps to Healing

Your spiritual health is determined by your relationship with Christ, and God's offer of salvation to you includes your physical health. You may wish to ask someone to pray with you. Agree together in prayer that GOD is going to answer. Stand on God's Word rather than trust in symptoms (Ja.1:6-8, NKJV). When praying for healing for someone in a public place, just simply believe GOD. After the prayer, ask them to walk and see if they are feeling better, walking better, whatever the case may be. Be sure to tell them that they will see the manifestation of their healing and for them to continue to believe GOD. **Get their name and phone number to follow up with them.**

Scriptures to Live by for Healing during Soulwinning:

(The following scriptures can be taken from any bible translation of the reader's choosing.)

Believe and confess salvation (Rom. 10:9-13, NIV; 1 Jn 1:8-9, NIV).

Agree with each other (Mat.18:9, NKJV)

Take God at His Word (Isa. 53:4-5, NIV).

Receive your healing by faith (Mk. 11:24, NIV).

Continue in the Lord, learning and growing (Ex.15:26, NIV).

If Symptoms Persist

If symptoms of a problem remain, they may indicate that there are barriers GOD wants to remove before He completes the healing. Barriers may include:

1. Harboring iniquity in your heart (Ps.66:18, NKJV). If our hearts don't condemn us we have confidence that God will answer our prayers (1 Jn. 3:21, NKJV).
2. Need to renounce cult or occult activity and false religious teachings (Deut.18:10-13, NIV).
3. Doubt, fear, anxiety, worry, unforgiveness, bitterness and other barriers to faith (Ja.4:7, NKJV and Eph. 6:11-12, NKJV).
4. Not having a whole-hearted desire to be healed. For example, illness may be like a security blanket or "old friend," you don't really want to lose. (I recall when Benny Hinn stated that a man did not want to be healed because he did not want to lose his disability check).
5. Stopping short of total healing after one symptom is gone, before the goal of total wholeness is reached.

6. God may be doing a parallel work in another person or situation, such as your spouse, relative, etc. If so, He may be bringing it all together, one thing bearing on the other. Begin praising GOD for the healing which will be manifested at a later date.

7. Need to be delivered from spiritual bondage. There is a sickness not unto death (Jn.11:4, NIV). This implies that there is sickness unto death. Similarly, there is a sin unto death and a sin not unto death (1 Jn 5:16-17, NIV). How do you know that yours is not a sickness or sin unto death? You don't. The question is not whether you have such sin. Instead, you and your prayer partner should try to determine what God wants you to do in this particular case. Expect the Holy Spirit to show you (Prov.16:3, NIV; Jn 16:12-15, NIV). Also read Scriptures that builds faith, assurance and gives direction.

Look at the scripture references I have given.

There may be a time when you and your prayer partner will feel that you have lost faith that God will heal you. If so, you can still ask God to work on your behalf. Don't limit Him! Commit yourself into His hands. Bind Satan in Jesus' name and praise God in His mercy and sovereignty; pray, expecting God to bless in His love. Seek out a Spirit-filled fellowship if you are not already part of one. We all need growth and edification that fellowship brings. It will help you learn to maintain your spiritual status and go from victory to victory.

Never advise anyone to cease taking medicine or medical treatment. If you believe God wants you to stop taking a medicine or treatment, do so in agreement with your doctor. You cannot act as an expert in such matters.

The prayer of thanksgiving and praise is acceptable to God. He answers before we ask. We can praise Him for His grace and love for us and for answering our prayers to heal. Remember that healing is sometimes a process, although a miracle of healing may be instantaneous.

HEALING SCRIPTURES:
(The following scriptures can be taken from any bible translation of the reader's choosing.)

Isaiah 53: 4-5

Romans 10:17 and John 8:31-32 -- FAITH

Deuteronomy 28:15-62, Galatians 3:13-- Redeemed from the curse of the law

John 15:7-- Abide in Christ

Philippians 4:13-19 -- A good confession

2 Timothy 1:7 -- A good confession

1 Peter 2:24, 25-- A good confession

2 Corinthians12:7-10 -- Beware of Satan's Messenger

Job 3:25 -- FEAR

Hebrews10:35, 36; Mark 11:24 -- Observe these-FAITH

Proverbs 4:20-22; Exodus 15:26—Observe these

John 11:4—Sickness not unto death

Feel comfortable about ministering healing at any time to anyone. GOD will use you. Have faith and believe-Nothing is impossible with GOD. Some people that may not want to

talk on the street will let you pray for them if they are sick or in pain, or hurting anywhere.

PRAY!

More Healing Scriptures: Look these up–BELIEVE GOD AND STUDY THESE SCRIPTURES SO YOU CAN MINISTER THEM TO OTHERS.

(The following scriptures can be taken from any bible translation of the reader's choosing.)

Isaiah 53:4-5

2 Corinthians 5:21; God declare the born–again person to be righteous in Christ.

Matthew 18:19

Mark 11:24

Romans 10:10; Your salvation includes your health.

1 John 5:14-15; He desires that we be saved, whole, healed.

Minister healing when needed. God can and will give you words of knowledge and wisdom. Speak what HE gives you, and let GOD use you especially if you know you have those gifts.

CHAPTER 19
Hope

People need to know that there is HOPE !

Hope is an essential part of life. If you think back over your life when things were so tough that you wanted to give up, no one was around and all hope was gone. Some folks have been there. Something had to happen for you to get up out of that rut and trust and believe GOD again. Perhaps you could call someone that will pray with you. There are wonderful ministries with prayer lines out there. I used to work for one of them. Or you dragged yourself to church and the preacher preached exactly what's going on in your life. And hope sprung up! The Holy Spirit in you rose up big, you got your vision back or your dream back and all became well again.

There's so many ways in everyday life that could destroy ones hope. And without hope we have nothing. Because the Bible says, that Faith is the substance of things hoped for, the evidence of things not seen. So, if we lose hope we lose faith. We have to have something to hope for!

Then imagine people out there on the street that may not have any hope. Perhaps they once did and lost it. And GOD sends you to tell them there is hope, even in their situations. You have just given that person a hint or a spark of light that they needed to continue on in life. You are a God-send! We are supposed to be. Every believer should be a 'God-send'. Instead of carrying gossip and strife, be a carrier of hope. Instead of sending a message of somebody else's business, send a message of hope. When a situation seems hopeless GOD will minister to you and also send someone to minister to you about holding on, help is on the way. There is always hope to be had. Grasp onto hope and give some away. There are thousands of people we pass daily that are in hopeless situations and GOD will use you to let them know that they do not have to give up. Jesus died for them and rose from the dead that they would have hope to live in this life, and the blessed assurance to live in the next life with Christ.

When people are seeking hope in difficult circumstances, but are experiencing anguish, despair and hopelessness, be encouraged in the Lord. GOD is the ultimate source for eternal hope. The Bible was written with the purpose of meeting your need (Rom. 15:4, NLT).

GOD has made promises to those who believe in Him. Every promise in the Bible, GOD says, is "Yea and Amen" in Christ. You have favor with GOD. He will see to it that you have favor with men. You need only learn to walk in that favor.

It is too often true that Christians experience far less GOD's best for them. However, God's promises are meant especially for Christians. Therefore, the place to start is with your relationship with God. It has been said that the entire Bible speaks of relationship, ours with God. That relationship starts with the new birth in Christ (Jn. 3:16, NKJV) which must be followed by spiritual growth. For there to be much spiritual growth, you also need to receive the Baptism of the Holy Spirit from Jesus (Lk. 11:13, AMP). The Holy Spirit produces the spiritual nature of GOD in you (Gal. 5:22-23, NIV). As you receive the spiritual nature of GOD, your old nature with its hopelessness (Gal. 5:19-21, NIV) is replaced. To be victorious in Christ, you also need God's armor and armament for life's battles (Eph. 6:10-18, NIV). (This is a must to make sure your armor is on daily). Finally, you need to begin practicing God's "spiritual laws" or "principles." Examine Christ's offer of "treasures in heaven" to the rich, young ruler (Mat. 19:21, NIV), or His offer of "living water," to the woman at the well (Jn. 4:1-15, NIV). Pray for and establish a new vision of what your lifestyle and relationships are to be like under God's authority.

As you study GOD'S word, you learn and experience God's full counsel for you, and your life takes on victory instead of defeat. You walk in faith and its results rather than constantly being defeated by the circumstances of life. Your prayers will become prayers of faith (and sure hope) rather than hopeless prayers.

GOOD TO KNOW--GOD has people to help you no matter what your needs --physical, spiritual, emotional, marital, or whatever. When talking to people in a public place about Christ they need to know sometimes depending on their circumstance, where they can get some help: Clothing for a job interview, food from a church cupboard, social services, etc. If you don't know right then and there but you know you can find out for them, get their phone number, etc. and commit to following up on things for them and getting back to them as soon as possible.

Your church has some of those ministries that can help them. God is a God of HOPE-Psalm 71. (Read it!).

Scripture references for Hope:

(The following scriptures can be taken from any bible translation of the reader's choosing.)

Romans 4:18-25	The Faith of Abraham
Psalm 23	God's assurances
2 Corinthians 4:7-9	Victorious Hope
Romans 5:5	Hope does not disappoint

Romans 8:24 (NKJV)

[24] For we are saved by hope, but hope that is seen is not hope: for why does one still hope for what he sees?

Acts 10:43 (KJV)

[43] To him give all the prophets witness, that through his name whosoever believeth in him shall receive remissions of sins.

John 14:27 (KJV)

[27] Peace I leave with you, my peace I give unto you: not as the world giveth, give I unto you. Let not your heart be troubled, neither let it be afraid.

1 John 1:3 (KJV)

[3] That which we have seen and heard declare we unto you, that ye also may have fellowship with us: and truly our fellowship is with the Father, and with his Son Jesus Christ.

Matthew 11:28-30 (KJV)

[28] Come unto me all ye that labor and are heavy laden and I will give you rest. [29] Take my yoke upon you, and learn of me; for I am meek and lowly in heart: and ye shall find rest unto your souls. [30] For my yoke is easy, and my burden is light.

Suggested reading:

"**Favor, the Road to Success**" By: Bob Buess

CHAPTER 20
PEACE-People need PEACE

Hope and peace are so important to be able to minister to someone on the street. Whether homeless or not! People even believers don't always know how to find peace in overwhelming circumstances. You need to have peace yourself before you can minister peace to others. Peace can radiate from others and yourself. Peace can be a lifestyle in any disastrous situation. "Peace! Be still!" is what JESUS said to the storm (Mk. 4:39, NIV).

When you can sleep at night through the storm, then you know that you did not create the storm. If you created the storm then find every way that you can to find peace. GOD is faithful to give you peace even when you have created the storm. He is just that kind of God.

Overwhelmed with inner conflict, fear, overwhelming temptation, anxiety, nervous tension, insomnia or anything like these can rob you of your peace. If you are experiencing one of these or several, you need to call on JESUS, who is the Prince of Peace. **If you need prayer right now, bow before GOD and ask HIM for HIS PEACE.**

Peace is a product of the Holy Spirit's actions (Gal. 5:22, NIV). It comes as you give preeminence (focus of attention) to the Prince of Peace (Isa. 26:3, NIV). Peace is a fruit of the Spirit.

How to Find Peace

The primary need for all people is salvation of their souls. When the Prince of Peace dwells within us, the Holy Spirit is able to produce His peace within us (Rom. 10:13, NKJV; 1 Jn. 1:9, NKJV; and Jn. 1:12, NKJV).

Upon asking Christ for the baptism (filling) of the Holy Spirit, you are eligible for all that God offers to those who trust Him. It is the Holy Spirit who empowers you for service, leads you into truth, comforts you and works mightily within you to give you victory over every situation of life which would rob you of your peace in God. When worry and wrong actions or attitudes are present, faith is absent. Born-again, Spirit filled Christians have received the spirit of adoption.

We know our Father in such an intimate way, and are known by Him, that we can call Him "Abba," or "Daddy." God's peace is included in His inheritance to His children.

God's Word promises that we are to be recipients of the fruit (qualities) of the Holy Spirit. Peace is one of those qualities (Gal. 5:22, NIV). Gaining peace is often a matter of changing our priorities. Honor and respect God instead of worrying over your lack of peace (Isa. 26:3, NKJV).

When you praise Him, you enthrone Him instead of the thoughts and emotions that take away your peace (Ps. 22:3, NIV). As you bless Him with your praise, He will bless you with His peace. No matter what may disturb you and cause your sense of well-being and peace to flee, you can give thanks and praise to God for it. Be assured that He intends to work even the most unlikely or seemingly impossible situation to the good of those who love Him, who are "called according to His purpose" (Eph. 5:20, NKJV; 1 Thess. 5:18, NKJV; and Rom. 8:28, NKJV).

Begin to thank and praise God in every need, and especially when you need assurance of His concern and saving power. Continue to honor God in praise until peace comes and joy springs up in your heart (Heb. 13:15, NIV). The joy and peace mean that God accepts your praise.

Isn't that the most awesome thing, that GOD accepts our praise?

PRAISE BREAK!

Finally, transform your thinking and actions. Start by intensively searching the Scriptures regarding freedom in Christ, authority as a Christian and how you can overcome the adversary, Satan. Faithfully attend your church, study God's Word and spend time daily in prayer and worshipful praise to God. His peace is yours as you seek Him.

Praying for a person who needs peace

In the authority of Jesus, bind demonic spirits. Command them to flee in Jesus' Name. Thank and praise God for His peace for you or for whomever you are praying for or with that needs the peace. Minister praise and thanksgiving to God regarding the fruit of the Spirit that has been given to you. PEACE! Thank you Lord for Your peace! Rejoice in the Lord in all circumstances. He wants to give you the desire of your heart.

What the Scripture says about Peace

Psalm 91:1(KJV)
He that dwells in the secret place of the Most High shall abide under the shadow of the Almighty.

Isaiah 26:3 (KJV)
Thou wilt keep him in perfect peace, whose mind is stayed on thee: because he trusts in thee.

Philippians 4:6 (KJV)
Be careful for nothing; but in everything by prayer and supplication with thanksgiving let your requests be made known unto God.

Matthew 6:31–33 (KJV)
Therefore take no thought…for your heavenly Father knows that you have need……But seek first the kingdom of God, and His righteousness, and all (your needs) shall be added unto you.

(The following scriptures can be taken from any bible translation of the reader's choosing.)
Romans 5:1-11 – We are inheritors of peace
Ephesians 2:14 – Christ is our peace
John 14:27 – Peace to be claimed
Isaiah 32:17, 48:18 – Righteousness and peace
Romans 8:6 – Holy Spirit and peace

ADDED TO THIS ARE THE DECLARATIONS OF THE FOLLOWING VERSES OF SCRIPTURE THAT ARE GOOD TO MEMORIZE:

Ephesians 2:8-9 (NKJV)
[8] For by grace you are saved through faith, and this is not of yourself, it is the gift of God; [9] not of works, lest anyone should boast.

Titus 3:5-7 (NIV)
[5] He saved us, not by works of righteousness that we have done, but on the basis of HIS mercy. He saved us through the washing of the new birth and the renewal of the Holy Spirit, [6] whom he poured out on us in full measure through Jesus Christ our Savior, [7] so that, having been justified by HIS grace, we become heirs having the hope of Eternal LIFE.

CHAPTER 21
Just a Review

Romans 4:1-5 (NKJV)
¹ What then shall we say that Abraham our ancestor according to the flesh? ² For if Abraham was declared justified by the works, he has something to boast about, but not before GOD. ³ For what does the scripture say? "Abraham believed God, and it was credited unto him as righteousness." ⁴ Now to the one who works, the wages are not counted as grace but as debt. ⁵ But to the one who does not work, but believes on Him who justifies the ungodly (that's us); his faith is accounted as righteousness.

No amount of human goodness is as good as GOD. GOD is perfect righteousness. Because of this, Habakkuk 1:13 (NKJV) tells us that GOD cannot have fellowship with anyone who does not have perfect righteousness. In order to be accepted by GOD, we must be as good as GOD. Before GOD, we all stand naked, helpless, and hopeless in ourselves. No amount of good living will get us to heaven, or give us eternal life. What then is the solution?

GOD'S Solution

GOD is not only perfect holiness (whose holy character we can never attain to on our own or by our works of righteousness) but HE is also perfect love and full of grace and mercy. Because of HIS love and grace, HE has not left us without hope and a solution.

"But GOD demonstrates his own love for us, in that while we were still sinners, CHRIST died for us." (Rom. 5:8, NKJV) This is the good news of the Bible, the message of the gospel. It's the message of the gift of GOD'S own Son who became man (the God-man), lived a sinless life, died on the cross for our sin, and was raised from the grave proving both the fact, HE is GOD'S SON and the value of HIS death for us as our substitute.

Romans 1:4 (NET)
[4] ...who was appointed the Son-of-GOD-in-power according to the Holy Spirit by the resurrection from the dead, Jesus Christ our Lord.

Romans 4:25 (NET)
[25] HE was given over because of our transgressions and was raised for the sake of our justification.

2 Corinthians 5:21(NET)
[21] GOD made the ONE who knew no sin to be sin for us, so that in HIM we would become the righteousness of GOD.

1 Peter 3:18 (NET)
[18] Because Christ also suffered once for sins, the just for the unjust, to bring you to GOD, by being put to death in the flesh but by being made alive in the spirit.

**GLORY TO GOD LET'S GIVE HIM
SOME PRAISE RIGHT THERE!**

CHAPTER 22
How Do We Receive God's SON ?

When we know this without a doubt we can lead an Atheist to Christ. Just get this down packed! Because of what Jesus Christ accomplished for us on the cross, the Bible states in 1 John 5:12 (NKJV):"He that has the SON has LIFE…". We can receive the SON, Jesus Christ as our Savior by personal faith, (GOD gives to every man/woman a measure of faith) by trusting in the person of Christ and HIS death for our sins.

John 1:12 (NKJV)
¹² But as many as received HIM, to them He gave the right to become children of God, to those who believe in His name…

John 3:16-18 (NIV)
¹⁶ For God so loved the world that HE gave HIS only begotten Son, that everyone who believes in HIM should not perish but will have eternal life. ¹⁷ For GOD did not send HIS Son into the world to condemn the world (*A VITALLY IMPORTANT PART OF THIS VERSE*) but that the world should be saved through HIM. ¹⁸ Whoever believes in him is not condemned, but whoever does not believe stands condemned already because they have not believed in the name of God's one and only Son.

This means that we must each come to GOD the same way.

1) As a sinner who recognizes his sinfulness.
2) Realizes no human works can result in salvation.
3) Relies totally on CHRIST alone by faith alone for our salvation.

If you would like to receive and trust Christ as your personal Savior, you may want to express your faith in Christ by a simple prayer acknowledging your sinfulness, accepting HIS forgiveness and putting your faith in Christ for your salvation:

DEAR LORD JESUS, COME INTO MY HEART, FORGIVE MY SINS, WASH ME IN YOUR BLOOD AND CLEANSE ME OF ALL UNRIGHTEOUSNESS. FILL ME WITH YOUR HOLY SPIRIT AND WRITE MY NAME IN YOUR LAMB'S BOOK OF LIFE. THANK YOU LORD FOR SAVING ME!

You may lead the individual person in the sinner's prayer and you can follow the pattern above.

Just an extra page to help you with your love walk

LOVE: SCRIPTURES TO LIVE BY
(*The following scriptures can be taken from any bible translation of the reader's choosing.*)

Read the entire book of 1 John

1 Corinthians 13:4–8	Characteristics associated with love
John 3:16	God's love revealed
1 John 4:7–14	God's love explained
Revelation 1:5	Christ's love is forever
Ephesians 2:4,5	God's love unearned

Matthew 22:37-38	Christ's Command to love
John 13:34-35	Love for each other proves we are God's people
Matthew 5:43-44	Love for enemies enjoined

You will know them by their fruit that they have love one for the other (Mt. 7:20, NKJV). This is the only scripture that tells us how we will know another believer. LOVE has to be a lifestyle and loving as GOD loves us-Agape Love! Practice it until it comes natural for you.

In a dream I saw myself standing on a platform. It did not look like a sanctuary, it looked like an auditorium, but there was a church service going on. I was standing in the middle of the platform behind the preacher that was a Bishop in the church. I could see the band in the corner of the platform playing. The bishop was preaching and I could see the bare left side of his rear-end. At that very moment, I began to be caught up in the Rapture, and I saw myself rising up from the platform into heaven and he was left behind. This is just an example of the following Scripture:

Matthew 7:20-23 (NKJV)

[20] Therefore by their fruits you will know them. [21] "Not everyone who says to Me, 'Lord, Lord,' shall enter the kingdom of heaven, but he who does the will of My Father in heaven. [22] Many will say to Me in that day, 'Lord, Lord, have we not prophesied in Your name, cast out demons in Your name, and done many wonders in Your name?' [23] And then I will declare to them, 'I never knew you; depart from Me, you who practice lawlessness!'

Bibliography

King James Version (KJV) Public Domain

Amplified Bible (AMP) Copyright © 2015 by The Lockman Foundation, La Habra, CA 90631.

The Common English Bible Study Bible (CEB). Nashville: The Common English Bible, 2011

English Standard Version (ESV) The Holy Bible, English Standard Version. ESV® Permanent Text Edition® (2016). Copyright © 2001 by Crossway Bibles, a publishing ministry of Good News Publishers.

The Message (MSG) Copyright © 1993, 1994, 1995, 1996, 2000, 2001, 2002 by Eugene H. Peterson

New American Standard Bible (NASB) Copyright © 1960, 1962, 1963, 1968, 1971, 1972, 1973, 1975, 1977, 1995 by The Lockman Foundation

Scripture quoted by permission. Quotations designated (NET©) are from the NET Bible® copyright ©1996-2016 by Biblical Studies Press, L.L.C. http://netbible.com All rights reserved.

New International Version (NIV) Holy Bible, New International Version®, NIV® Copyright ©1973, 1978, 1984, 2011 by Biblica, Inc.® Used by permission.

Dr. Joe Temple **Crown of Rejoicing: Soul-Winner's Crown** http://www.livingbiblestudies.org/study/JT2/003.html

CBN : The Christian Broadcasting Network

Something About the Author...

Missionary Evangelist Linda D. Casraiss was born and raised in Philadelphia, PA. In December 1981, she gave her life to Christ and became a born-again Christian. She has traveled the world as a Missionary to China, Russia, the Philippines, Jamaica, Israel, and throughout the United States of America. She is the CEO/Founder of *GateKeeper's Ministry International* and *GateKeeper's Ministry International Radio Station* that the Lord has taken global where twenty-some nations tune in as she hosts Prophets, Apostles, Evangelists, Pastors, and Ministers. She is the CEO/Founder of *CremationPlus*, a business derived from the Lord's vision of how she arranged her mother's Memorial. Linda has an Associate's Degree in Journalism from the Philadelphia Community College in Philadelphia, Pennsylvania, and a Bachelor's Degree in English and Communications from Cheyney University in Cheyney, Pennsylvania.

She was a teacher and trainer of the Sing, Spell, Read and Write Adult Literacy Program in Philadelphia, Pennsylvania for American Family Services. In 1981, she was a volunteer and later employed by the Christian Broadcasting Network. She was promoted to Supervisor at the CBN Philadelphia Counseling Center.

She teaches Soul Winning classes from her manual, "How to Win a Soul to Christ and Make it a Lifestyle".

She is the mother of one daughter, Shaune' and two grandsons, Xavier and River.

Linda is an ordained Deacon. She is a prayer-warrior. She enjoys feeding the homeless, conducting hospital visits, praying for the sick, reading books on the Prophetic, on Dreams and Visions, and the Bible. And she enjoys walking, quiet time before the Lord and working out.

Linda is a Dreamer. Look for her next book entitled, DIARY OF A DREAMER.

To contact Linda, send an email to wealthywells@gmail.com.

Printed in the United States
By Bookmasters